Nerf

by Julie Murray

Abdo Kids Jumbo is an Imprint of Abdo Kids
abdobooks.com

abdobooks.com

Published by Abdo Kids, a division of ABDO, P.O. Box 398166, Minneapolis, Minnesota 55439.

Printed in the United States of America, North Mankato, Minnesota.

102025

012026

THIS BOOK CONTAINS
RECYCLED MATERIALS

Photo Credits: Alamy, Getty Images, Shutterstock, ©JeepersMedia p.7,p.13/CC BY 2.0
©The Strong National Museum of Play, Rochester, New York, p.17

Production Contributors: Teddy Borth, Jennie Forsberg, Grace Hansen
Design Contributors: Candice Keimig, Pakou Moua

Library of Congress Control Number: 2025936512

Publisher's Cataloging-in-Publication Data

Names: Murray, Julie, author.

Title: Nerf / by Julie Murray

Description: Minneapolis, Minnesota : Abdo Kids, 2026 | Series: Toy mania! | Includes online resources and index.

Identifiers: ISBN 9798384907589 (lib. bdg.) | ISBN 9798384908289 (ebook) | ISBN 9798384908630 (read-to-me ebook)

Subjects: LCSH: NERF toys--Juvenile literature. | War toys--Juvenile literature. | Toy guns--Juvenile literature. | Sports--Equipment and supplies--Juvenile literature. | Hasbro Entertainment (Firm)--Juvenile literature. | Toys--Juvenile literature. | Toys--History--Juvenile literature.

Classification: DDC 790.1--dc23

Table of Contents

Nerf

Nerf products have entertained kids and adults for more than 55 years. From foam balls to Nerf Blasters, it's Nerf or nothin' in the toy world!

MEGA

Play Ball in the House!

The toy company Parker Brothers released the Nerf ball in 1969. It was the first indoor ball. It flew off the shelves and sold more than 4.5 million its first year!

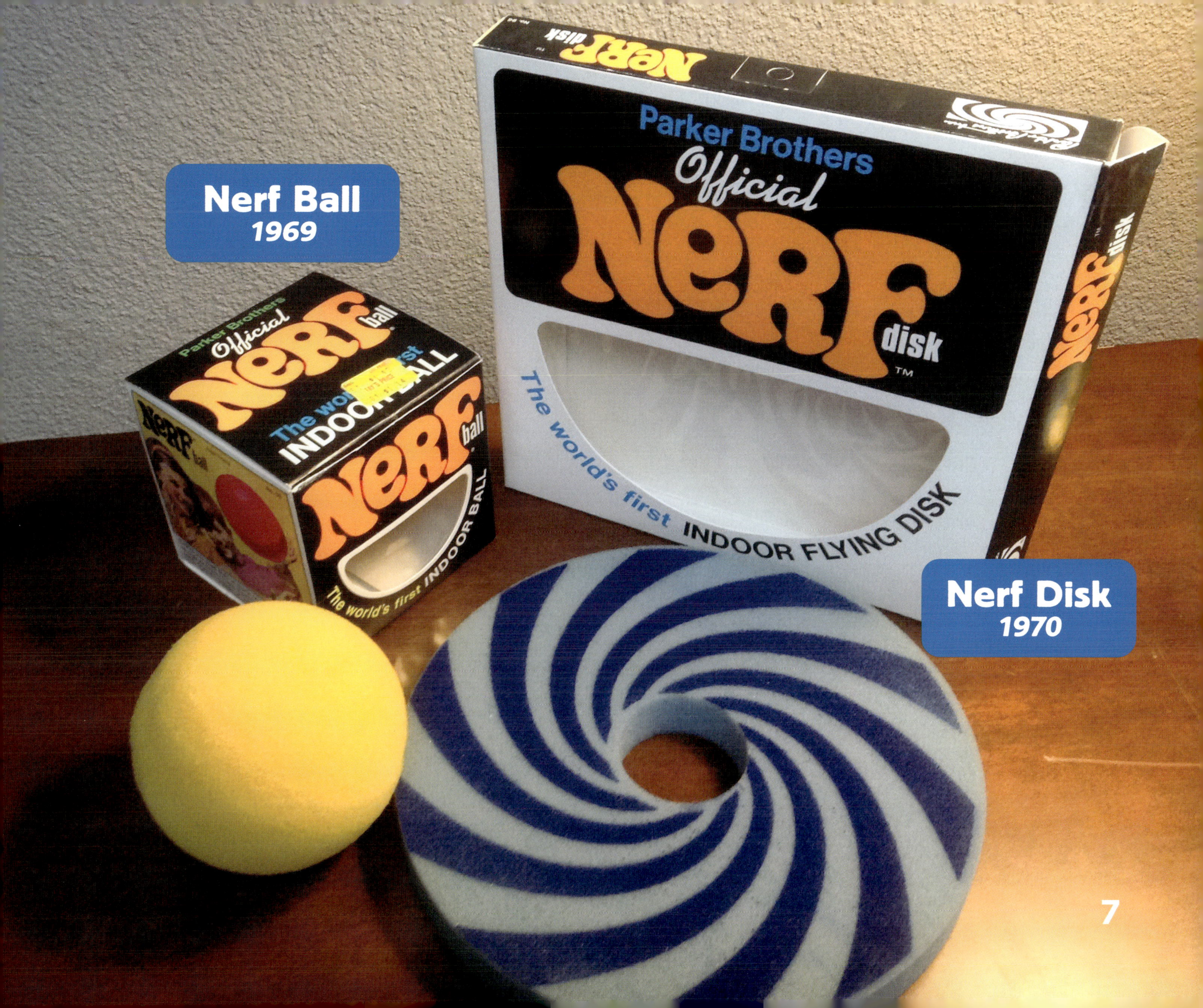
Nerf Ball
1969
Parker Brothers Official NERF ball
INDOOR BALL
NERF ball
The world's first INDOOR BALL
Parker Brothers
Official
NERF disk
The world's first INDOOR FLYING DISK
Nerf Disk
1970

Reyn Guyer and his team of toy **inventors** created the Nerf ball. But before that, they came up with a caveman game where players threw foam rocks at other players.

Reyn Guyer

Throwing the soft foam rocks was the best part of the game. So, Guyer and his team decided to **scrap** the caveman game and make a foam ball instead.

The team took their idea to Parker Brothers, who agreed to a deal. At first, people were **skeptical** about a ball that didn't bounce. But everyone loved the foam ball that could be used inside!

NERF ball
INDOOR BALL
The world's first INDOOR BALL

More Nerf products quickly followed. The Nerf football was one of the biggest hits! It was released in 1972. It was soft and easy to grip.

NFL Star Peyton Manning

NFL Star
Archie
Manning

NFL Star
Eli
Manning

Nerf's a Blast!

The Blast-a-Ball came out in 1989. The hand-pumped air blaster shot out foam balls. It was an early **model** of the Nerf Blaster.

-BALL GAME
POP!
·2 BLASTERS ·4 SAFE, SOFT BALLS
T 'EM, DODGE 'EM, CATCH 'EM GAME · PROJECTS BALLS UP TO 30 FEET

In 1991, Hasbro took over the toy brand. The same year, the Nerf Blaster **debuted**. Today, there are more than 20 different Blaster lines. They shoot balls, darts, disks, and arrows.

NERF
ELITE 2.0
PHOENIX
PHOENIX CS-6
12x
10X
MEGA
TRI-BREAK
GEAR UP PACK
NERF
LIONFURY
16x
6+
NERF
6+
RACER
NERF
FORTNITE
DUAL PACK
LP & FLINT-KNOCK
x6
NERF
8+
6x
MINECRAFT
FIREBRAND
12x
будинок іграшок
ELITE
DEMOLISHER 2-IN-1

More than 100 different Nerf products have been made since the brand's **debut**. Nerf continues to make new toys that keep kids and adults active, entertained, and safe!

•AGENT BOW
•ARC AGENT SECRET
•GEHEIMNIS BOGEN
•AGENT BOW
SECRETS & SPIES
•ELECTRONIC SIGHT
•VISEUR ÉLECTRONIQUE
•ELEKTRONISCHES VISIER
•MIRA ELECTRÓNICA
25m
•FIRES ARROWS!
•VRAIES FLÈCHES !
•SCHIESST PFEILE AB!
•¡LANZA FLECHAS!
3X
NerfRebelle.com
Hasbro

More Facts

- Some off-road vehicles use protective foam padding called "nerf bars." This is where Nerf got its name.
- Nerf sells more than 40 million Nerf Blasters each year!
- Nerf was **inducted** into the National Toy Hall of Fame in 2023.

Glossary

debut – a first appearance; to present to an audience for the first time.

inducted – brought in as a member.

inventor – one who invents. To invent is to create something new.

model – a particular type or style of a product.

scrap – to get rid of.

skeptical – having or showing doubt.

Index

Visit **abdokids.com** to access crafts, games, videos, and more!

Use Abdo Kids code

TNK7589

or scan this QR code!